WOOD PELLET SMOKER AND GRILL COOKBOOK FOR BEGINNERS

THE ULTIMATE WOOD PELLET SMOKER AND GRILL COOKBOOK, USE THIS ULTIMATE GUIDE FOR SMOKING MEAT, FISH, GAME, AND VEGETABLES

CONTENTS

Introduction

Where there is a smoke, there is a flavor. Smoking meat or making BBQ is not only a means of cooking but for some individuals and classy enthusiasts, this is a form of Art! Or dare I say a form of lifestyle! Enthusiasts all around the world have been experimenting and dissecting the secrets of perfectly smoked meat for decades now, and in our golden age, perhaps they have cracked it up completely!In our age, the technique of Barbequing or Smoking meat has been perfected to such a level, that a BBQ Grill is pretty much an essential amenity found in all backyard or sea-beach parties!

This is the drinking fountain for the more hip and adventurous people, who prefer to have a nice chat with their friends and families while smoking up a few batches of Burger Patty for them to enjoy. But here's the thing, while this art might seem as a very easy form of cooking which only requires you to flip meats over and over! Mastering it might be a little bit difficult if you don't know have the proper information with you. This guide is an essential book for beginners who want to smoke meat without needing expert help from others. This book offers detailed guidance obtained by years of smoking meat, includes clear instructions and step-by-step directions for every recipe. This is the only guide you will ever need to professionally smoke a variety of food. The book includes full-color photographs of every finished meal to make your job easier. Whether you are a beginner meat smoker or looking to go beyond the basics, the book gives you the tools and tips you need to start that perfectly smoked meat.

Smoking is something has withstood the test of time, it will continue to stand the test of time for years to come. Not only is it a method to preserve your catch or kill, but it's also one of if not the best-tasting food there is.

Chapter-1 BEEF

Chipotle Honey Smoked Beef Roast

(Cooking Time 4 Hours 20 Minutes)

Ingredients for 10 Servings

- Beef roast (5-lbs., 2.3-kg.)

The Rub

- Vegetable oil – 2 tablespoons
- Black pepper – 1 ½ tablespoons
- Salt – 1 ½ tablespoons
- Brown sugar – ¾ tablespoon
- Onion powder – ¾ tablespoon
- Mustard – 1 teaspoon
- Garlic powder – 1 ½ teaspoons
- Chipotle powder – 1 ½ teaspoons

The Glaze

- Honey – ½ cup
- Water – 2 tablespoons
- Minced garlic – 1 ½ tablespoons

The Heat

- Hickory wood pellets

Method

1. Place the rub ingredients—vegetable oil, black pepper, salt, brown sugar, onion powder, mustard, garlic powder, and chipotle powder in a bowl then mix until combined.
2. Rub the beef roast with the spice mixture then set aside.
3. Plug the wood pellet smoker and place wood pellet inside the hopper. Turn the switch on.
4. Set the “Smoke” setting and prepare the wood pellet smoker for indirect heat.
5. Wait until the smoke is ready and adjust the temperature to 275°F (135°C).
6. Once the wood pellet smoker has reached the desired temperature, place the seasoned beef roast directly on the grate inside the wood pellet smoker and smoke for 2 hours.
7. In the meantime, combine honey, water, and minced garlic in a bowl then stir until incorporated.
8. After 2 hours, take the beef roast out of the wood pellet smoker and place on as sheet of aluminum foil.
9. Leave the wood pellet smoker on and adjust the temperature to 300°F (149°C).
10. Baste the beef roast with the glaze mixture then wrap it with the aluminum foil.
11. Return the wrapped beef roast to the wood pellet smoker then smoke for another 2 hours.
12. Once the internal temperature of the smoked beef roast has reached 165°F (74°C), remove it from the wood pellet smoker.
13. Let the smoked beef roast rest for about 10 minutes then unwrap it.
14. Transfer the smoked beef roast to a serving dish then serve.
15. Enjoy!

Lemon Chili Smoked Beef Brisket

(COOKING TIME 4 HOURS 10 MINUTES)

INGREDIENTS FOR 10 SERVINGS

- Beef brisket (4.5-lbs., 2-kg.)

THE RUB

- Lemon juice – 3 tablespoons
- Chili powder – ¼ cup
- Salt – 1 ½ tablespoons
- Garlic powder – 2 tablespoons
- Cayenne – 2 teaspoons
- Pepper – 2 teaspoons

THE HEAT

- Alder wood pellets

METHOD

1. Combine chili powder with salt, garlic powder, cayenne, and pepper then mix well.
2. Rub the beef brisket with lemon juice then sprinkle the dry spice mixture over the beef brisket.
3. Plug the wood pellet smoker and fill the hopper with wood pellets. Turn the switch on.
4. Set the "Smoke" setting and prepare the wood pellet smoker for indirect heat.
5. Adjust the temperature of the wood pellet smoker to 275°F (135°C) and wait until it reaches the desired temperature.
6. Place the seasoned beef brisket directly on the grate in the wood pellet smoker and smoke for approximately 3 hours or until the internal temperature has reached 125°F (52°C).
7. After 2 hours, take the beef brisket out of the wood pellet smoker and transfer to a sheet of aluminum foil.
8. Wrap the beef brisket with the aluminum foil then return it back to the wood pellet smoker.
9. Smoke the wrapped beef brisket for another 2 hours or until the internal temperature has reached 165°F (74°C).
10. Once it is done, remove the wrapped smoked beef brisket from the wood pellet smoker and let it rest for about 10 minutes.
11. Unwrap the smoked beef brisket then cut into slices.
12. Serve and enjoy.

Smoked Beef Ribs Sweet Barbecue

(COOKING TIME 3 HOURS 40 MINUTES)

INGREDIENTS FOR 10 SERVINGS

- Beef ribs (6-lbs., 2.7-kg.)

THE RUB

- Brown sugar – ¼ cup
- Paprika – 2 ½ tablespoons
- Mustard – 1 ½ teaspoons
- Onion powder – 1 ½ tablespoons
- Garlic powder – 1 ½ tablespoons
- Basil – ¾ tablespoons
- Bay leaves – 1 teaspoon
- Coriander – ½ tablespoons
- Thyme – ½ teaspoon
- Black pepper – 1 teaspoon
- Cumin – ¼ teaspoon
- Salt – 2 tablespoons

THE GLAZE

- Ketchup – 1 cup
- Apple cider vinegar – ¼ cup
- Soy sauce – ¼ cup
- Worcestershire sauce – ¼ cup
- Minced garlic – 1 ½ tablespoons
- Mustard – 1 ½ tablespoons
- Black pepper – ¾ teaspoon
- Salt – ½ teaspoon

THE HEAT

- Mesquite wood pellets

Method

1. Remove the excess fat from the beef ribs then set aside.
2. Combine the rub ingredients in a bowl.
3. Place brown sugar, paprika, mustard, onion powder, garlic powder, basil, bay leaves, coriander, thyme, black pepper, cumin, and salt in the bowl then mix until combined.
4. Rub the beef ribs with the spice mixture then set aside.
5. Plug the wood pellet smoker and fill the hopper with wood pellets. Turn the switch on.
6. Set the "Smoke" setting and prepare the wood pellet smoker for indirect heat.
7. Wait until the smoke has reached 225°F (107°C) then put the seasoned beef ribs in the wood pellet smoker.
8. Smoke the beef ribs for approximately an hour and a half or until the internal temperature has reached 125°F (52°C).
9. In the meantime, pour ketchup in a bowl then add apple cider vinegar, soy sauce, and Worcestershire sauce to the bowl.
10. Season the glaze mixture with minced garlic, mustard, black pepper, and salt then stir well.
11. After an hour and a half, take the beef ribs out of the wood pellet smoker and transfer to a disposable aluminum pan.
12. Glaze the beef ribs with the glaze mixture then cover the disposable aluminum pan with aluminum foil.
13. Adjust the temperature of the wood pellet smoker to 250°F (121°C) and return the wrapped beef ribs to the wood pellet smoker.
14. Smoke the beef ribs for approximately 2 hours or until the internal temperature has reached 165°F (74°C).
15. Once the smoked beef ribs are done, remove it from the wood pellet smoker and let it rest for about 15 minutes.
16. Unwrap the smoked beef ribs from the wood pellet smoker and transfer to a serving dish.
17. Serve and enjoy.

Smoked Beef Steak with Cilantro Lime Sauce

(COOKING TIME 3 HOURS 20 MINUTES)

INGREDIENTS FOR 10 SERVINGS

- Flank steak (4-lbs., 1.8-kg.)

THE MARINADE

- Red wine – ½ cup
- Vegetable oil – ½ cup
- Black pepper – ½ tablespoon
- Salt – 1 tablespoon
- Soy sauce – ¼ cup
- Worcestershire sauce – ¼ cup
- Minced garlic – 3 tablespoons
- Lemon juice – 3 tablespoons

THE SAUCE

- Chopped cilantro – 2 cups
- Minced garlic – 3 tablespoons
- Olive oil – 1 cup
- Red wine vinegar – ½ cup
- Fresh limes – 2
- Diced onion – 2 tablespoons
- Black pepper – 2 teaspoons
- Salt – ½ tablespoon

The Heat

- Hickory wood pellets

Method

1. Pour red wine and vegetable oil in a zipper-lock plastic then season black pepper, salt, salt, soy sauce, Worcestershire sauce, minced garlic, and lemon juice. Stir well until incorporated.
2. Add the flank steak to the zipper-lock plastic bag then shake until the flank steak is completely seasoned.
3. Marinate the flank steak for 8 hours and store in the fridge to keep it fresh.
4. After 8 hours, plug the wood pellet smoker and fill the hopper with wood pellets. Turn the switch on.
5. Set the "Smoke" setting and prepare the wood pellet smoker for indirect heat.
6. Adjust the temperature to 225°F (107°C) and when it reaches the desired temperature, place the seasoned flank steak in the wood pellet smoker.
7. Smoke the flank steak for 3 hours or until the internal temperature has reached 180°F (82°C).
8. Once the smoked flank steak is done, remove from the wood pellet smoker and quickly wrap with aluminum foil. Let it rest for approximately 15 minutes.
9. In the meantime, place cilantro, minced garlic, and diced onion in a blender then pour olive oil and red wine vinegar over the ingredients.
10. Season with black pepper and salt then blend until smooth.
11. Transfer the sauce mixture to a saucepan then bring to a simmer over low heat.
12. Remove the sauce from heat then let it cool.
13. Cut the limes into halves then squeeze the juice over the sauce.
14. Unwrap the smoked flank steak and transfer to a serving dish.
15. Serve with sauce then enjoy.

Spicy Smoked Rib Eye with Bourbon Butter Sauce

(Cooking time 3 hours 30 minutes)

Ingredients for 10 servings

- Beef rib eye (4-lbs., 1.8-kg.)

The Rub

- Cumin – 2 tablespoons
- Paprika – 2 tablespoons
- Garlic powder – 2 tablespoons
- Onion powder – 2 tablespoons
- Chili powder – 2 tablespoons
- Brown sugar – 2 tablespoons
- Salt – 1 ½ tablespoons
- Cayenne pepper – ½ tablespoon
- Black pepper – ½ tablespoon

The Sauce

- Butter – 1 cup
- Minced garlic – 2 tablespoons
- Bourbon – ¼ cup
- Diced onion – 2 tablespoons
- Minced parsley – 2 tablespoons
- Salt – ½ teaspoon
- Black pepper – 1 teaspoon

THE HEAT

- Mesquite wood pellets

METHOD

1. Rub the beef rib eye with cumin, paprika, garlic powder, onion powder, chili powder, brown sugar, salt, cayenne pepper, and black pepper then set aside. Let it rest for about 30 minutes.
2. In the meantime, place the entire sauce ingredients—butter, minced garlic, bourbon, diced onion, minced parsley, salt, and black pepper in a mixing bowl then using a mixer blend until smooth and creamy.
3. Transfer the bourbon butter sauce to a container with a lid then store in the refrigerator.
4. Plug the wood pellet smoker and fill the hopper with wood pellets. Turn the switch on.
5. Set the "Smoke" setting and prepare the wood pellet smoker for indirect heat.
6. Adjust the temperature to 250°F (121°C) and when it reaches the desired temperature, place the seasoned beef rib eye in the wood pellet smoker.
7. Smoke the beef rib eye for approximately 3 hours or until the internal temperature has reached 145°F (63°C) for medium doneness. If you like it well done, you may add about 30 minutes of smoking time or until the internal temperature has reached 165°F (74°C).
8. Once the smoked beef rib eye is done, remove from the wood pellet smoker and transfer to a serving dish.
9. Drop the bourbon butter sauce over the smoked beef rib eye then serve.
10. Enjoy!

Chapter-2 PORK

Savory Smoked Pork Belly with Sweet Honey Glaze

(Cooking Time 3 Hours 45 Minutes)

Ingredients for 10 servings

- Pork Belly (3.5-lbs., 1.6-kg.)

The Rub

- Brown sugar – ¼ cup
- Salt – 1 ½ tablespoons
- Paprika – 2 ½ tablespoons
- Black pepper – 1 ½ tablespoons
- Chili powder – 2 tablespoons
- Onion powder – 1 ½ tablespoons
- Garlic powder – 1 tablespoon

The Glaze

- Brown sugar – ¼ cup
- Honey – ½ cup

The Heat

- Apple wood pellets

Method

1. Combine the entire rub ingredients—brown sugar, salt, paprika, black pepper, chili powder, onion powder, and garlic powder in a bowl. Mix until incorporated.
2. Rub the pork belly with the spice mixture then set aside.
3. Next, plug the wood pellet smoker and place wood pellet inside the hopper. Turn the switch on.
4. Set the "Smoke" setting and prepare the wood pellet smoker for indirect heat.
5. Adjust the temperature to 275°F (135°C) and once it reaches the desired temperature, place the seasoned pork belly in the wood pellet smoker.
6. Smoke the pork belly for an hour then take it out.
7. Glaze the pork belly with honey then sprinkle brown sugar over the pork belly.
8. Wrap the glazed pork belly with aluminum foil then return it back to the wood pellet smoker.
9. Smoke the wrapped pork belly for 2 hours and a half or until the internal temperature has reached 195°F (91°C).
10. Once it is done, remove the smoked pork belly from the wood pellet smoker and let it rest for about 10 minutes.
11. Unwrap the smoked pork belly then transfer to a serving dish.
12. Cut the smoked pork belly into slices then serve.
13. Enjoy.

Juicy Smoked Pork Ribs with Gingery Barbecue Sauce

(Cooking Time 5 Hours 15 Minutes)

Ingredients for 10 Servings

- Pork Ribs (6-lbs., 2.7-kg.)

The Rub

- Apple Juice – ½ cup
- Brown sugar – ½ cup
- Salt – 2 tablespoons
- Black pepper – 1 teaspoon
- Garlic powder – 2 tablespoons
- Onion powder – 1 tablespoon
- Oregano – 2 tablespoons
- Cayenne pepper – 1 teaspoon
- Chili powder – 2 tablespoons

The Glaze

- Vegetable oil – ½ cup
- Onion powder – 1 tablespoon
- Garlic powder – 1 tablespoon
- Ginger – ½ tablespoon
- Ketchup – 1 cup
- Apple juice – ¾ cup
- Oyster sauce – 3 tablespoons
- Apple cider vinegar – 2 tablespoons
- Mustard – 1 teaspoon

The Heat

- Hickory wood pellets

METHOD

1. Combine the dry rub ingredients—brown sugar, salt, black pepper, garlic powder, onion powder, oregano, cayenne pepper, and chili powder in a bowl. Mix until incorporated.
2. Baste the pork ribs with apple juice then sprinkle dry rub mixture over the pork ribs. Set aside.
3. Plug the wood pellet smoker and place wood pellet inside the hopper. Turn the switch on.
4. Set the "Smoke" setting and prepare the wood pellet smoker for indirect heat.
5. Adjust the temperature to 225°F (107°C) and wait until it reaches the desired temperature.
6. Place the seasoned pork ribs in the wood pellet smoker and smoke for 3 hours.
7. In the meantime, combine vegetable oil with ketchup, apple juice, oyster sauce, and apple cider vinegar in a bowl then seasoned with onion powder, garlic powder, ginger, and mustard. Stir until incorporated.
8. After 3 hours of smoking, take the pork ribs out of the wood pellet smoker and brush with the glaze mixture.
9. Wrap the pork belly with aluminum foil then return it back to the wood pellet smoker.
10. Smoke the pork ribs for another 2 hours or until the internal temperature of the smoked pork ribs has reached 165°F (74°C).
11. Once it is done, remove the smoked pork ribs from the wood pellet smoker and let it rest for about 15 minutes.
12. Unwrap the smoked pork ribs then transfer to a serving dish.
13. Serve and enjoy.

Smoked Pork Tenderloin with Honey Apple Marinade

(COOKING TIME 3 HOURS 10 MINUTES)

INGREDIENTS FOR 10 SERVINGS

- Pork Tenderloin (3-lbs., 1.4-kg.)

THE MARINADE

- Apple juice – 1 cup
- Honey – ½ cup
- Brown sugar – ½ cup
- Thyme – 3 tablespoons
- Black pepper – ¾ tablespoon
- Chili powder – 1 teaspoon
- Italian seasoning – ½ teaspoon
- Onion powder – 1 teaspoon

THE HEAT

- Apple wood pellets

METHOD

1. Combine the marinade ingredients in a container in a bowl.
2. Pour the apple juice and honey in a container then add brown sugar, thyme, black pepper, chili powder, Italian seasoning, and onion powder to it. Stir well.
3. Place the pork tenderloin in the container then marinate the pork tenderloin for at least 2 hours. Store in the fridge to keep it fresh.
4. After 2 hours, remove the marinated pork from the fridge and thaw at room temperature.
5. Next, plug the wood pellet smoker and place wood pellet inside the hopper. Turn the switch on.
6. Set the "Smoke" setting and prepare the wood pellet smoker for indirect heat.

7. Adjust the temperature to 225°F (107°C) and wait until it reaches the desired temperature.
8. Place the seasoned pork ribs in the wood pellet smoker and smoke for 3 hours.
9. Once the internal temperature has reached 145°F (63°C), take the smoked pork out of the wood pellet smoker and transfer to a serving dish.
10. Serve and enjoy.

Smoked Pork Roast Garlic with Rosemary

(Cooking Time 4 Hours 10 Minutes)

Ingredients for 10 Servings

- Pork Roast (4.5-lbs., 2-kg.)

The Rub

- Minced garlic – ¾ cup
- Black pepper – 3 tablespoons
- Brown sugar – 3 tablespoons
- Salt – 2 tablespoons

The Liquid

- Apple juice – ¼ cup

The Topping

- Chopped rosemary – 1 cup

The Heat

- Apple wood pellets

METHOD

1. Plug the wood pellet smoker and place wood pellet inside the hopper. Turn the switch on.
2. Set the "Smoke" setting and prepare the wood pellet smoker for indirect heat.
3. Adjust the temperature to 275°F (135°C) and wait until it reaches the desired temperature.
4. In the meantime, combine minced garlic with black pepper, brown sugar, and salt in a bowl.
5. Rub the pork roast with the spice mixture then place in a disposable aluminum pan.
6. Drizzle apple juice over the pork roast and sprinkle chopped rosemary on top.
7. Once the smoke is ready, place the disposable aluminum pan in the wood pellet smoker.
8. Smoke the pork roast for 2 hours then cover the disposable aluminum pan with aluminum foil.
9. Return the pork roast to the wood pellet smoker and smoke for another 2 hours.
10. Once the internal temperature of the smoked pork roast has reached 170°F (77°C), remove the disposable aluminum pan from the wood pellet smoker.
11. Let the smoked pork roast rest for approximately 10 minutes then transfer to a serving dish.
12. Serve and enjoy.

Juicy Smoked Pulled Pork BBQ

(Cooking Time 5 Hours 10 Minutes)

Ingredients for 10 servings

- Pork Butt (5-lbs., 2.3-kg.)

The Brine

- Water – 4 ½ cups
- Apple cider – 3 ½ cups
- Salt – ½ cup
- Brown sugar – ¾ cup
- Bay leaves – 2
- Cayenne pepper – 1 teaspoon

The Rub

- Onion powder – 1 ½ tablespoons
- Smoked paprika – ½ teaspoon
- Garlic powder – 1 tablespoon
- Chili powder – ¾ tablespoon
- Salt – 1 tablespoon
- Pepper – ¾ tablespoon
- Cayenne powder – 1 ½ teaspoons
- Dry mustard – 2 teaspoons
- Cumin – ¾ tablespoon
- Brown sugar – ¾ cup

The Sauce

- Yellow mustard – 1 cup
- Honey – ¾ cup
- Apple cider vinegar – ¼ cup
- Ketchup – 3 tablespoons
- Brown sugar – 1 ½ tablespoons
- Worcestershire sauce – 1 tablespoon
- Butter, melted – 3 tablespoons
- Nutmeg – ½ teaspoon

The Heat

- Apple wood pellets

Method

1. Combine the rub ingredients—onion powder, smoked paprika, garlic powder, chili powder, salt, pepper, cayenne powder, dry mustard, cumin, and brown sugar in a bowl then mix well.
2. Take about 2 tablespoons of the spice mixture then place in a container.
3. Add salt, brown sugar, bay leave, and cayenne pepper to the container then pour water and apple cider vinegar over the spices. Stir until incorporated.
4. Next, put the pork butt in the container and soak in the brine overnight. Cover the container with the lid and store in the fridge to keep it fresh.
5. In the morning, remove the pork butt from the fridge and take it out from the brine. Thaw at room temperature.
6. In the meantime, plug the wood pellet smoker and place wood pellet inside the hopper. Turn the switch on.
7. Set the "Smoke" setting and prepare the wood pellet smoker for indirect heat.
8. Adjust the temperature to 225°F (107°C) and wait until it reaches the desired temperature.
9. Rub the pork butt with the remaining spice mixture and once the wood pellet smoker is ready, place the seasoned pork butt in it.
10. Smoke the pork butt for 2 hours then transfer to a disposable aluminum pan.
11. Cover the disposable aluminum pan with aluminum foil then return it back to the wood pellet smoker.

12. Smoke the pork butt for another 3 hours or until the internal temperature has reached 165°F (74°C).
13. Remove the smoked pork butt from the wood pellet smoker then let it rest for about 10 minutes.
14. Meanwhile, combine yellow mustard with honey, apple cider vinegar, ketchup, brown sugar, Worcestershire sauce, melted butter, and nutmeg in a bowl then stir until incorporated. Set aside.
15. Unwrap the smoked pork butt then using a fork shred into pieces.
16. Drizzle the sauce over the shredded smoked pork then mix well.
17. Transfer the shredded smoked pork to a serving dish and serve.
18. Enjoy!

Chapter-3 LAMB

Oregano Spiced Smoked Lamb Rib with Spicy barbecue

(Cooking Time 5 Hours 20 Minutes)

Ingredients for 10 servings

- Lamb ribs (5-lbs., 2.3-kg.)

The Rub

- Chili powder – 1 tablespoon
- Garlic powder – ½ tablespoon
- Oregano – 1 teaspoon
- Salt – 1 ½ teaspoons
- Smoked sweet paprika – 1 ½ teaspoons
- Coriander – 1 teaspoon
- Dry mustard powder – 1 ½ teaspoons
- Allspice – 1 ½ teaspoons
- Pepper – 1 teaspoon
- Canola oil – 3 tablespoons

The Glaze

- Ketchup – 2 ½ cups
- Molasses – ¾ cup
- Apple cider vinegar – ¼ cup
- Canola oil – 2 tablespoons
- Minced garlic – 2 tablespoons
- Chili powder – 1 teaspoon
- Salt – ¼ teaspoon
- Pepper – ½ teaspoon

The Heat

- Apple wood pellets

Method

1. Place the entire rub ingredients—chili powder, garlic powder, oregano, salt, sweet smoked paprika, coriander, dry mustard powder, allspice, pepper, and canola oil in a bowl. Stir the spices until well combined.
2. Rub the lamb ribs with the spice mixture and ensure the lamb ribs are completely coated with the spice mixture.
3. Wrap the seasoned lamb ribs with aluminum foil then let it rest for at least 6 hours or overnight. Store in the fridge to keep it fresh.
4. After 6 hours, remove the seasoned lamb ribs from the fridge and thaw at room temperature.
5. Next, plug the wood pellet smoker and place wood pellet inside the hopper. Turn the switch on.
6. Set the "Smoke" setting and prepare the wood pellet smoker for indirect heat.
7. Wait until the smoke is ready and adjust the temperature to 225°F (107°C).
8. Once the wood pellet smoker is ready, unwrap the lamb ribs and place in the wood pellet smoker. Smoke for 2 hours.
9. In the meantime, combine ketchup, molasses, apple cider vinegar, canola oil, minced garlic, chili powder, salt, and pepper in a saucepan then bring to a simmer over very low heat.
10. Stir the mixture until incorporated then remove from heat.
11. After 2 hours of smoking, baste the lamb ribs with barbecue mixture then continue smoking for another 3 hours. Baste the lamb ribs with barbecue mixture once every 30 minutes.
12. Once it is done or the internal temperature of the smoked lamb ribs has reached 165°F (74°C), remove it from the wood pellet smoker.
13. Arrange the smoked lamb ribs with the barbecue glaze on a serving dish then serve.
14. Enjoy!

Savory Smoked Lamb Leg with Green Cilantro Salsa

(Cooking Time 5 hours 10 minutes)

Ingredients for 10 servings

- Boneless lamb leg (4-lbs., 1.8-kg.)

The Rub

- Minced garlic – 4 tablespoons
- Salt – 1 ½ tablespoons
- Ground black pepper – 1 tablespoon
- Oregano – 1 ½ tablespoons
- Thyme – 1 teaspoon
- Ginger – ½ teaspoon
- Canola oil – 3 tablespoons

The Salsa

- Garlic – 4 cloves
- Diced onion – ¼ cup
- Green chili – 1 teaspoons
- Chopped fresh cilantro – ½ cup
- Sugar – ½ teaspoon
- Canola oil – 2 tablespoons
- Chicken broth – ¾ cup
- Lemon juice – 2 tablespoons

The Heat

- Alder wood pellets

Method

1. Baste the boneless lamb leg with canola oil then rub with minced garlic, salt, ground black pepper, oregano, thyme, and ginger.
2. Plug the wood pellet smoker and fill the hopper with wood pellets. Turn the switch on.
3. Set the "Smoke" setting and prepare the wood pellet smoker for indirect heat.
4. Adjust the temperature of the wood pellet smoker to 225°F (107°C) and wait until it reaches the desired temperature.
5. Once the wood pellet smoker is ready, place the seasoned lamb in the wood pellet smoker and smoke for 5 hours.
6. Next, place garlic, diced onion, green chili, chopped fresh cilantro, and sugar in a blender.
7. Pour canola oil, chicken broth, and lemon juice into the blender then blend until smooth and incorporated.
8. Transfer the cilantro mixture to a saucepan then bring to a simmer over very low heat.
9. Once the smoked lamb leg is done or the internal temperature has reached 165°F (74°C), remove it from the wood pellet smoker.
10. Place the smoked lamb on a serving dish then cut into thick slices.
11. Top with green cilantro salsa then serve.
12. Enjoy!

Juicy Mint Pulled Smoked Lamb Shoulder

(Cooking Time 6 hours 10 minutes)

Ingredients for 10 servings

- Boneless Lamb Shoulder (6-lbs., 2.7-kg.)

The Rub

- Garlic powder – 2 tablespoons
- Onion powder – 2 tablespoons
- Nutmeg – ½ teaspoon
- Salt – 1 teaspoon
- Pepper – ½ teaspoon

The Liquid

- Brown sugar – ¼ cup
- Beer – ¼ cup
- Chopped mint leaves – ¼ cup
- Apple cider vinegar – 1 ½ tablespoons
- Salt – ¼ teaspoon
- Pepper – ½ teaspoon

THE HEAT

- Hickory wood pellets

METHOD

1. Rub the lamb shoulder garlic powder, onion powder, nutmeg, salt, and pepper. Mix the spices until well combined.
2. Plug the wood pellet smoker and fill the hopper with wood pellets. Turn the switch on.
3. Set the "Smoke" setting and prepare the wood pellet smoker for indirect heat.
4. Once the wood pellet smoker is ready, set the temperature to 250°F (121°C) and place the seasoned lamb shoulder in it. Smoke the lamb shoulder for 2 hours.
5. In the meantime, combine pour beer and apple cider vinegar into a disposable aluminum pan then season with brown sugar, salt, and pepper. Stir the mixture until incorporated.
6. Add chopped mint leaves to the disposable aluminum pan then stir until just combined.
7. After 2 hours of smoking, remove the lamb shoulder from the smoker then transfer to the prepared disposable aluminum pan.
8. Return the lamb shoulder to the wood pellet smoker and smoke for another 4 hours.
9. Once the smoked lamb shoulder is done, remove from the wood pellet smoker and transfer to a cutting board.
10. Using a knife or a fork shred the smoked lamb shoulder then place on a serving dish.
11. Drizzle the liquid over the shredded smoked lamb then stir a bit.
12. Serve and enjoy.

Smoked Lamb Pistachio Crumbles with Sweet Apricot

(Cooking time 6 hours 10 minutes)

Ingredients for 10 servings

- Lamb Ribs (5-lbs., 2.3-kg.)

The Rub

- Garlic – 7 cloves
- Mint leaves – ¼ cup
- Canola oil – 3 tablespoons
- Salt – 1 teaspoon
- Cumin – 1 ½ teaspoons
- Fennel – ¾ teaspoon
- Coriander – ¾ teaspoon
- Black peppercorns – ¾ teaspoon
- Roasted pistachio – ½ cup
- Brown sugar – 3 tablespoons

The Glaze

- Apricot jam – ¾ cup
- Canola oil – 2 tablespoons

The Heat

- Mesquite wood pellets

METHOD

1. Place pistachio in a food processor then add garlic and mint leaves.
2. Season with salt, cumin, fennel, coriander, black peppercorns, and brown sugar then drizzle canola oil into the food processor. Process until smooth and incorporated.
3. Discard the excess fat from the lamb ribs then spread the pistachio mixture all over the lamb ribs.
4. Cover the seasoned lamb ribs with aluminum foil then let it rest overnight. Store in the refrigerator to keep it fresh.
5. In the morning, remove the seasoned lamb ribs from the refrigerator and thaw at room temperature.
6. Plug the wood pellet smoker and fill the hopper with wood pellets. Turn the switch on.
7. Set the "Smoke" setting and prepare the wood pellet smoker for indirect heat.
8. Adjust the temperature to 225°F (107°C) and wait until the wood pellet smoker has reached the desired temperature.
9. Unwrap the seasoned lamb ribs and place in the wood pellet smoker.
10. Smoke the lamb ribs for 5 hours or until the internal temperature has reached 165°F (74°C).
11. Remove the smoked lamb ribs from the wood pellet smoker and place on a plate.
12. Quickly combine the glaze ingredients—apricot jam and canola oil then baste the smoked lamb ribs with the mixture.
13. Wrap the smoked lamb ribs with aluminum foil then let it rest for approximately an hour.
14. Unwrap the smoked lamb ribs and transfer to a serving dish.
15. Serve and enjoy.

Oregano Coffee Smoked Lamb with Espresso Glaze

(COOKING TIME 5 HOURS 10 MINUTES)

INGREDIENTS FOR 10 SERVINGS

- Lamb Ribs (4-lbs., 1.8-kg.)

THE RUB

- Ground coffee beans – 2 tablespoons
- Salt – 1 teaspoon
- Sweet paprika powder – 2 teaspoons
- Cayenne pepper – 1 tablespoon
- Brown sugar – 1 ½ tablespoons
- Oregano – 1 teaspoon
- Garlic powder – 1 ½ teaspoons
- Onion powder – 1 teaspoon
- Black pepper – ¾ teaspoon
- Coriander – ¾ teaspoon

THE GLAZE

- Beef broth – ½ cup
- Espresso – ½ cup
- Maple syrup – ½ cup
- Worcestershire sauce – 1 tablespoon
- Olive oil 2 tablespoons

The Heat

- Cherry wood pellets

Method

1. Combine the rub ingredients—ground coffee beans, salt, sweet paprika powder, cayenne pepper, brown sugar, oregano, garlic powder, onion powder, black pepper, and coriander in a bowl. Stir the spice mixture until incorporated.
2. Rub the lamb with the spice mixture then let it rest.
3. Plug the wood pellet smoker and fill the hopper with wood pellets. Turn the switch on.
4. Set the "Smoke" setting and prepare the wood pellet smoker for indirect heat.
5. Once the smoke is ready, place the seasoned lamb in the wood pellet smoker. Smoke the lamb with the bone side down for 2 hours and a half.
6. Meanwhile, pour beef broth, espresso, maple syrup, Worcestershire sauce, and olive oil in a bowl then stir all the liquid until incorporated.
7. After 2 hours and a half of smoking, remove the lamb from the wood pellet smoker.
8. Keep the wood pellet smoker on and set the temperature to 225°F (107°C)
9. Glaze the lamb with the espresso glaze mixture then wrap with aluminum foil.
10. Return the wrapped lamb to the wood pellet smoker and smoke for another 2 hours and a half.
11. Once the internal temperature has reached 165°F (74°C), remove the smoked lamb from the wood pellet smoker and let it cool for a few minutes.
12. Unwrap the smoked lamb then transfer to a serving dish.
13. Serve and enjoy.

Chapter-4 HAM

Aromatic Clove Smoked Ham with Sweet Glaze

(Cooking Time 3 Hours 40 Minutes)

Ingredients for 10 Servings

- Spiral Sliced Ham (4-lbs., 1.8-kg.)

The Spices

- Salt – 1 teaspoon
- Pepper – 1 teaspoon
- Ground clove – 1 teaspoon

The Glaze

- Brown sugar – ½ cup
- Honey – ¼ cup
- Olive oil – 2 tablespoons
- Dijon mustard – ½ tablespoon
- Worcestershire sauce – 1 teaspoon
- Cinnamon – ½ teaspoon
- Ginger – ½ teaspoon
- Pepper – ¼ teaspoon
- Garlic powder – ½ teaspoon
- Onion powder – ½ teaspoon
- Mustard – ½ teaspoon
- Cayenne pepper – ¼ teaspoon

The Heat

- Maple wood pellets

METHOD

1. Plug the wood pellet smoker and place wood pellet inside the hopper. Turn the switch on.
2. Set the "Smoke" setting and prepare the wood pellet smoker for indirect heat.
3. Adjust the temperature to 225°F (107°C) and wait until the wood pellet smoker is ready.
4. Combine salt with pepper and ground cloves then stir the spices until mixed.
5. Sprinkle the spice mixture over the ham then place the ham in the wood pellet smoker. Smoke the ham for an hour and a half.
6. In the meantime, combine honey with olive oil then add brown sugar, Dijon mustard, Worcestershire sauce, cinnamon, ginger, pepper, garlic powder, onion powder, mustard, and cayenne pepper. Stir the mixture until incorporated.
7. After an hour and a half, increase the temperature to 300°F (148°C) and baste the ham with the honey mixture.
8. Smoke the ham for another 2 hours or until the internal temperature has reached 140°F (60°C)
9. Once it is done, remove the smoked ham from the wood pellet smoker and transfer to a serving a serving dish.
10. Serve and enjoy!

Rosemary Garlic Smoked Ham Barbecue

(COOKING TIME 3 HOURS 40 MINUTES)

INGREDIENTS FOR 10 SERVINGS

- Skinless ham (5-lbs., 2.3-kg.)

THE BRINE

- Water – 1 quart
- Apple cider – 1 quart
- Cider vinegar – 1 cup
- Salt – ½ cup
- Brown sugar – ½ cup
- 1 bay leaf

THE RUB

- Fresh chopped rosemary – ¼ cup
- Minced garlic – 1 ½ tablespoons
- Salt – 1 tablespoon

THE GLAZE

- Apple cider vinegar – ¼ cup
- Soy sauce – ½ tablespoon
- Worcestershire sauce – ½ tablespoon
- Ketchup – ¼ cup
- Brown sugar – 2 tablespoons
- Smoked paprika – 1 teaspoon
- Cumin – ½ teaspoon
- Black pepper – ½ teaspoon

The Heat

- Apple wood pellets

Method

1. Combine water with apple cider, cider vinegar, salt, and brown sugar then stir the liquid until incorporated.
2. Add ham to the brine mixture then put a bay leaf into the brine.
3. Soak the ham for at least 5 hours, or overnight. Store in the fridge to keep it fresh.
4. In the morning, remove the ham from the fridge and thaw at room temperature.
5. Take the ham from the brine then wash and rinse it.
6. Cut rosemary into very small dices then combine with salt and minced garlic. Rub the ham with the rosemary mixture.
7. Plug the wood pellet smoker and fill the hopper with wood pellets. Turn the switch on.
8. Set the "Smoke" setting and prepare the wood pellet smoker for indirect heat.
9. Adjust the temperature of the wood pellet smoker to 250°F (121°C) and wait until it reaches the desired temperature.
10. Once the wood pellet smoker is ready, place the seasoned ham in the wood pellet smoker. Smoke the ham for approximately an hour.
11. In the meantime, combine the glaze ingredients—apple cider vinegar, soy sauce, Worcestershire sauce, ketchup, brown sugar, smoked paprika, cumin, and black pepper in a bowl. Stir the mixture until incorporated.
12. After an hour of smoking, baste ham with the glaze mixture then continue smoking for another 2 hours.
13. Baste the ham with the glaze mixture once every 30 minutes and check if the internal temperature has reached 165°F (74°C).
14. Once it is done, remove the smoked ham from the wood pellet smoker and place on a flat surface. Let the smoked ham cool for approximately 30 minutes.
15. Cut the smoked ham into slices then serve.

Double Apricot Sweet Smoked Ham

(Cooking Time 3 hours 10 minutes)

Ingredients for 10 servings

- Ham (5-lbs., 2.3-kg.)

The Rub

- Brown sugar – ¼ cup
- Mustard – 1 tablespoon
- Ground clove – ½ teaspoon
- Apricot preserves – ¼ cup

The Glaze

- Apricot preserves – ¼ cup
- Apricot syrup – ½ cup
- Ketchup – 2 tablespoons
- Soy sauce – 1 tablespoon
- Molasses – ½ tablespoon

The Heat

- Hickory wood pellets

Method

1. Combine brown sugar, mustard, ground cloves, and apricot preserves in a bowl then stir the mixture until well mixed.
2. Rub ham with the apricot mixture then let it rest for a few minutes.
3. Plug the wood pellet smoker and fill the hopper with wood pellets. Turn the switch on.
4. Set the "Smoke" setting and prepare the wood pellet smoker for indirect heat.
5. Adjust the temperature to 225°F (107°C) and place the ham in the wood pellet smoker. Smoke the ham for 2 hours.

6. Mix apricot preserves, apricot syrup, ketchup, soy sauce, and molasses in a bowl then stir the mixture until incorporated.
7. After 2 hours of smoking, baste the ham with the apricot glaze then continue smoking for an hour.
8. Once it is done, remove the smoked ham from the wood pellet smoker and baste with the remaining apricot mixture.
9. Wrap the smoked ham with aluminum foil then let it rest for 30 minutes.
10. After 30 minutes, unwrap the smoked ham and cut into thin slices.
11. Serve and enjoy.

Smoked Ham Cinnamon Flavor

(Cooking time 4 hours 10 minutes)

Ingredients for 10 servings

- Ham (4-lbs., 1.8-kg.)

The Brine

- Water – 1 quart
- Salt – ½ cups
- Brown sugar – ¼ cup
- Minced garlic – 2 tablespoons
- Mustard – 1 tablespoon
- Coriander – ½ tablespoon
- Bay leaf - 1

The Glaze

- Orange juice – 1 ½ cups
- Lemon juice – 2 tablespoons
- Cumin – ½ tablespoon
- Paprika – 1 teaspoon
- Grated orange zest – 1 teaspoon
- Brown sugar – ½ cup
- Cinnamon – ½ teaspoon

The Heat

- Hickory wood pellets

Method

1. Add salt, brown sugar, minced garlic, mustard, coriander, and bay leaf to the water then stir the brine until incorporated.
2. Soak the ham in the brine for 6 hours or overnight and store in the fridge to keep it fresh.

3. Remove the ham from the fridge then thaw at room temperature. Wash and rinse the ham.
4. Plug the wood pellet smoker and fill the hopper with wood pellets. Turn the switch on.
5. Set the "Smoke" setting and prepare the wood pellet smoker for indirect heat.
6. Adjust the temperature to 200°F (93°C) and wait until the wood pellet smoker has reached the desired temperature.
7. Once the smoke is ready, place ham in the wood pellet smoker and smoke for 2 hours.
8. Combine orange juice with lemon juice, cumin, paprika, grated orange juice, brown sugar, and cinnamon then stir the glaze until incorporated.
9. After 2 hours of smoking, baste the ham with the glaze mixture and smoke for another 2 hours. Baste the ham with the remaining glaze once every 30 minutes.
10. When the smoked ham is done, remove from the wood pellet smoker and transfer to a flat surface.
11. Let it cool for a few minutes then cut into thick slices.
12. Serve and enjoy.

Refreshing Smoked Ham with Butter Champagne Sauce

(Cooking time 3 hours 10 minutes)

Ingredients for 10 servings

- Ham (4-lbs., 1.8-kg.)

The Glaze

- Honey Mustard – ¼ cup
- Brown sugar – ¼ cup
- Orange juice – ¼ cup

The Sauce

- Butter – ½ cup
- Orange juice – 1 cup
- Champagne – ½ cup
- Brown sugar – ½ cup
- Ginger – ½ teaspoon
- Grated orange zest – ½ teaspoon

The Heat

- Mesquites wood pellets

Method

1. Combine the glaze ingredients—honey mustard, brown sugar, and orange juice in a bowl then baste the ham with the glaze mixture.
2. Plug the wood pellet smoker and fill the hopper with wood pellets. Turn the switch on.
3. Set the "Smoke" setting and prepare the wood pellet smoker for indirect heat.
4. Once the smoke is ready, adjust the temperature to 225°F (107°C) and place ham in the wood pellet smoker. Smoke the ham for 2 hours.

5. In the meantime, place butter in a saucepan then melt over very low heat.
6. Stir in orange juice, champagne, brown sugar, ginger, and grated orange juice then bring to a simmer. Remove from heat.
7. After 2 hours of smoking, remove the ham from wood pellet smoker and place in a disposable aluminum pan.
8. Drizzle champagne butter sauce over the ham then return to the wood pellet smoker.
9. Smoke the ham for another 2 hours or until the internal temperature has reached 165°F (74°C).
10. Once the smoked ham is done, remove from the wood pellet smoker and place on a flat surface. Let it cool for a few minutes.
11. Cut the smoked ham into thin slices then place on a serving dish.
12. Drizzle the sauce over the smoked ham then serve.
13. Enjoy!

Chapter-5 POULTRY

Lemon Garlic Smoked Chicken

(Cooking Time 3 Hours 10 Minutes)

Ingredients for 10 servings

- Whole Chicken (3-lbs., 1.4-kg.)

The Brine

- Salt – ½ cup
- Brown sugar – 1 cup
- Water – 3 ½ liters

The Rub

- Minced garlic – ¼ cup
- Garlic powder – 2 tablespoons
- Lemon juice – 3 tablespoons
- Paprika – 2 ½ tablespoons
- Chili powder – 2 tablespoons
- Thyme – ¾ tablespoon
- Cayenne – 2 tablespoons
- Salt – 1 tablespoon
- Black pepper – 2 tablespoons

The Filling

- Chopped onion – 1 cup
- Garlic – 5 cloves
- Thyme – 5 sprigs

The Heat

- Mesquite wood pellets

Method

1. Stir in salt and brown sugar to the water then mix until completely dissolved.
2. Put the chicken in the brine then soak overnight. Store in fridge to keep it fresh.
3. On the next day, remove the chicken from the fridge then wash and pat it dry. Set aside.
4. Combine the rub ingredients—minced garlic, garlic powder, lemon juice, paprika, chili powder, thyme, cayenne, salt, and black pepper in a bowl then mix well.
5. Rub the chicken with the spice mixture then fill the cavity with chopped onion, garlic, and thyme.
6. Next, plug the wood pellet smoker and place wood pellet inside the hopper. Turn the switch on.
7. Set the "Smoke" setting and prepare the wood pellet smoker for indirect heat.
8. Adjust the temperature to 225°F (107°C) and place the seasoned whole chicken in the wood pellet smoker.
9. Smoke the chicken for approximately 3 hours or until the internal temperature has reached 165°F (74°C).
10. Once it is done, remove the smoked chicken from the wood pellet smoker and let it sit for about 10 minutes.
11. Place the smoked chicken on a serving dish then serve.

Sweet Honey Smoked Brown Turkey

(Cooking Time 4 Hours 40 Minutes)

Ingredients for 10 servings

- Whole Turkey (6-lbs., 2.7-kg.)

The Rub

- Salt – 5 tablespoons
- Brown sugar – 5 tablespoons
- Thyme – 1 tablespoon
- Chopped rosemary – 1 tablespoon
- Sage – 1 tablespoon
- Black pepper – 2 ½ teaspoons
- Garlic powder – 2 teaspoons

The Glaze

- Raw honey – 1 cup
- Brown sugar – 3 tablespoons
- Apple Cider Vinegar – 2 tablespoon
- Mustard – ¾ tablespoon
- Salt - 1 teaspoon
- Pepper – 2 teaspoons

The Heat

- Maple wood pellets

Method

1. Combine the rub ingredients—salt, brown sugar, thyme, chopped parsley, sage, black pepper, and garlic powder in a bowl then mix well.
2. Rub the turkey with the spice mixture then let it rest for a few minutes.
3. Next, plug the wood pellet smoker and place wood pellet inside the hopper. Turn the switch on.

4. Set the "Smoke" setting and prepare the wood pellet smoker for indirect heat.
5. Adjust the temperature to 375°F (191°C) and place the seasoned turkey in the wood pellet smoker.
6. Smoke the turkey for approximately 20 minutes or until the skin of the turkey turns into brown.
7. After that, reduce the temperature into 325°F (163°C) and continue smoking the turkey for approximately 4 hours or until the internal temperature has reached 165°F (74°C).
8. Quickly place brown sugar, apple cider vinegar, mustard, salt, and pepper in a bowl then pour raw honey over the mixture. Stir until combined.
9. Baste the smoked turkey with the honey mixture then return it back to the wood pellet smoker.
10. Smoke the turkey for another 20 minutes then remove from the wood pellet smoker.
11. Let the smoked turkey rest for a few minutes then cut into small pieces.
12. Serve and enjoy!

Spicy Smoked Chicken Garlic

(Cooking Time 3 Hours 10 Minutes)

Ingredients for 10 Servings

- Whole Chicken (3-lbs., 1.4-kg.)

The Rub

- Salt – 1 teaspoon
- Paprika – 1 teaspoon
- Garlic powder – 1 ½ teaspoons
- Black pepper – 1 ½ teaspoons
- Red chili flakes – 2 teaspoons
- Cayenne pepper – ½ teaspoon
- Thyme – ¾ teaspoon
- Oregano – ½ teaspoon
- Brown sugar – 3 tablespoons

The Heat

- Apple wood pellets

Method

1. Rub the chicken with salt, paprika, garlic powder, black pepper, red chili flakes, cayenne pepper, thyme, oregano, and brown sugar.
2. Wrap the seasoned chicken with plastic wrap then let it rest for approximately an hour. Store in the fridge to keep it fresh.
3. Plug the wood pellet smoker and place wood pellet inside the hopper. Turn the switch on.
4. Set the "Smoke" setting and prepare the wood pellet smoker for indirect heat.
5. Take the chicken out of the fridge and thaw at room temperature. Discard the plastic wrap.
6. Once the wood pellet smoker is ready, place the seasoned chicken in the wood pellet smoker and smoke for approximately 10 minutes.

7. Adjust the temperature to 225°F (107°C) and continue smoking the chicken for approximately 3 hours or until the internal temperature has reached 165°F (74°C).
8. Once it is done, remove the smoked chicken from the wood pellet smoker and place on a serving dish.
9. Cut the smoked chicken into pieces then serve.
10. Enjoy!

Hot Smoked Shredded Chicken with Sweet Sticky Sauce

(Cooking Time 3 Hours 10 Minutes)

Ingredients for 10 servings

- Boneless Chicken breast (3-lbs., 1.4-kg.)

The Rub

- Paprika – 3 tablespoons
- Chili powder – 3 tablespoons
- Thyme – 1 ½ tablespoons
- Garlic powder – 1 ½ tablespoons
- Onion powder – 1 ½ tablespoons
- Cayenne – 3 tablespoons
- Salt – 1 ½ tablespoons
- Black pepper – 1 ½ tablespoons

The Sauce

- Honey – ½ cup
- Maple syrup – ¼ cup
- Brown sugar – 2 tablespoons

The Heat

- Maple wood pellets

METHOD

1. Combine the rub ingredients—paprika, chili powder, thyme, garlic powder, onion powder, cayenne, salt, and black pepper in a bowl then mix well.
2. Score the chicken breast and rub with the spice mixture. Let it rest for a few minutes.
3. Next, plug the wood pellet smoker and place wood pellet inside the hopper. Turn the switch on.
4. Set the "Smoke" setting and prepare the wood pellet smoker for indirect heat.
5. Once the wood pellet smoker is ready, set the temperature to 225°F (107°C) and place the chicken breast in the wood pellet smoker.
6. Smoke the chicken for an hour then transfer to a disposable aluminum pan.
7. Quickly combine honey with maple syrup then stir until incorporated.
8. Drizzle half of the honey mixture over the chicken breast then sprinkle brown sugar on top.
9. Flip the chicken breast then coat the other side of the chicken with honey mixture and brown sugar.
10. Place the disposable aluminum pan with chicken inside in the wood pellet smoker then smoke for about 2 hours.
11. After 2 hours, check if the internal temperature has reached 165°F (74°C). Add more time if it is necessary.
12. Once the chicken is done, take the disposable aluminum pan from the wood pellet smoker and let it rest for a few minutes.
13. Using a fork or a sharp knife shred the smoked chicken then place on a serving dish.
14. Drizzle the liquid over the smoked chicken then stir a bit.
15. Serve and enjoy.

Natural White Smoked Chicken Breast

(Cooking Time 2 Hours 15 Minutes)

Ingredients for 10 Servings

- Boneless Chicken breast (4.5-lbs., 2 -kg.)

The Injection

- Vegetable oil – 3 tablespoons
- Chicken broth – ¼ cup
- Worcestershire sauce – 2 tablespoons
- Salt – ¾ tablespoon
- Garlic powder – 1 ½ teaspoons
- Onion powder – 1 ½ teaspoons
- Bay leaf – ¾ teaspoon
- Thyme – ¾ teaspoon
- Sage – ¾ teaspoon
- Black pepper – ¾ teaspoon

The Rub

- Salt – 2 tablespoons
- Minced garlic – 3 tablespoons
- Minced ginger – 1 tablespoon
- Lemon juice – 3 tablespoons

The Heat

- Pecan wood pellets

Method

1. Pour vegetable oil and chicken broth into a bowl then season with Worcestershire sauce, salt, garlic powder, onion powder, bay leaf, thyme, sage, and black pepper. Stir the liquid until incorporated.
2. Fill an injector with the liquid mixture then inject the chicken breast at several places.
3. After that, combine the rub ingredients—salt, minced garlic, minced ginger, and lemon juice in a bowl. Stir the spices until well mixed.
4. Rub the chicken breast with the spice mixture then let it rest for an hour.
5. Next, plug the wood pellet smoker and place wood pellet inside the hopper. Turn the switch on.
6. Set the "Smoke" setting and prepare the wood pellet smoker for indirect heat.
7. Once the wood pellet smoker is ready, set the temperature to 250°F (121°C) and place the chicken breast in the wood pellet smoker.
8. Smoke the chicken for 2 hours and once the internal temperature has reached 165°F (74°C), remove the smoked chicken from the wood pellet smoker.
9. Quickly wrap the smoked chicken with aluminum foil then let it rest for approximately an hour or so.
10. After an hour, unwrap the smoked chicken then cut into thick slices.
11. Arrange the sliced smoked chicken on a serving dish then serve immediately.
12. Enjoy!

Chapter-6 FISH

Simple Sweet Maple Smoked Salmon

(COOKING TIME 2 HOURS 10 MINUTES)

INGREDIENTS FOR 10 SERVINGS

- Salmon (6-lbs., 2.7-kg.)

THE BRINE

- Water – 5 cups
- Brown sugar – 1 ¼ cups
- Salt - ½ cup

THE GLAZE

- Olive oil – 2 tablespoons
- Maple Syrup – 1 cup

THE HEAT

- Cherry wood pellets

METHOD

1. Pour water into a container then stir in brown sugar and salt to the water. Stir the mixture until combined.
2. Put the salmon in the brine mixture then soak for approximately 12 hours. Store in the fridge to keep it fresh.
3. After 12 hours, remove the salmon from the brine and rinse it. Using a paper towel, pat it dry.
4. Plug the wood pellet smoker and place wood pellet inside the hopper. Turn the switch on.
5. Set the "Smoke" setting and prepare the wood pellet smoker for indirect heat.
6. Adjust the temperature to 200°F (93°C) and place the salmon in the wood pellet smoker.

7. Spray the salmon with olive oil then smoke for approximately 2 hours.
8. Baste the salmon with maple syrup once every 30 minutes and wait until the internal temperature of the smoked salmon has reached 145°F (63°C).
9. Remove the smoked salmon from the wood pellet smoker and transfer to a serving dish.
10. Serve and enjoy.

Lemon Orange Smoked Tuna

(Cooking Time 3 Hours 45 Minutes)

Ingredients for 10 Servings

- Tuna Fillet (4-lbs., 1.8-kg.)

The Brine

- Water – 4 cups
- Brown sugar – 1 cup
- Kosher salt – ¼ cup
- Grated orange zest – 1 teaspoon
- Grated lemon zest – 1 teaspoon

The Heat

- Pecan wood pellets

Method

1. Combine brown sugar with salt, grated orange zest, and grated lemon zest then mix well.
2. Pour water over the mixture then stir until incorporated.
3. Put the tuna in the brine mixture then soak for approximately 6 hours. Store in the refrigerator to keep it fresh.
4. Next, plug the wood pellet smoker and place wood pellet inside the hopper. Turn the switch on.
5. Set the "Smoke" setting and prepare the wood pellet smoker for indirect heat.
6. In the meantime, remove the tuna from the refrigerator and take it out from the brine.
7. Wash and rinse the tuna then using a paper towel, pat it dry.
8. Once the wood pellet smoker is ready, place the tuna on the rack and smoke for 30 minutes.
9. After 30 minutes, adjust the temperature into 225°F (107°C) and smoke the tuna for approximately 2 hours or until the internal temperature of the smoked tuna has reached 145°F (63°C).
10. Once the smoked tuna is done, remove from the wood pellet smoker and transfer to a serving dish.
11. Serve and enjoy with vegetable salad.

Smoked Whole Trout Soy Black Pepper

(COOKING TIME 2 HOURS 10 MINUTES)

INGREDIENTS FOR 10 SERVINGS

- Whole Trout (5-lbs., 2.3-kg.)

THE BRINE

- Water – 6 cups
- Salt – ½ cup
- Brown sugar – ½ cup
- Soy sauce – ¾ cup
- Black pepper – 1 ½ tablespoons

THE HEAT

- Oak wood pellets

METHOD

1. Place the entire brine ingredients—water, salt, brown sugar, soy sauce, and black pepper in a container then stir until incorporated.
2. Put the trout in the brine mixture and soak for at least 2 hours. Store in the fridge to keep it fresh.
3. After 2 hours, remove the trout from the fridge and take it out of the brine.
4. Wash and rinse the trout then pat it dry using a paper towel. Set aside.
5. Plug the wood pellet smoker and place wood pellet inside the hopper. Turn the switch on.
6. Set the "Smoke" setting and prepare the wood pellet smoker for indirect heat.
7. Once the wood pellet smoker is ready, place the seasoned trout on the rack inside the wood pellet smoker.
8. Smoke the trout for approximately 2 hours or until the internal temperature of the smoked trout has reached 145°F (63°C). The smoked trout will start to flake.
9. Once the smoked trout is done, remove from the wood pellet smoker and transfer to a serving dish.
10. Serve and enjoy.

Buttery Smoked Halibut with Tahini Dip

(Cooking Time 1 Hour 10 Minutes)

Ingredients for 10 Servings

- Halibut fillet (5-lbs., 2.3-kg.)

The Rub

- Butter – ½ cup
- Minced garlic – 3 teaspoons
- Salt – ¾ teaspoon
- Pepper – ¾ teaspoon
- White wine – ¾ cup

The Dip

- Lemon juice – ½ cup
- Tahini paste – 1 cup
- Mayonnaise – ½ cup
- Vegetable oil – ½ cup

The Heat

- Alder wood pellets

Method

1. Melt the butter then combine with minced garlic, salt, and pepper.
2. Pour white wine over the mixture then stir until incorporated.
3. Rub the halibut fillet with the butter mixture then let it rest for approximately an hour. Store in the fridge to keep it fresh.
4. After an hour, remove the seasoned halibut from the fridge and let it thaw at room temperature.
5. In the meantime, plug the wood pellet smoker and place wood pellet inside the hopper. Turn the switch on.
6. Set the "Smoke" setting and prepare the wood pellet smoker for indirect heat.

7. Adjust the temperature to 225°F (107°C) and once it reaches the desired temperature, place the seasoned halibut in the wood pellet smoker.
8. Smoke the halibut for approximately an hour or until the internal temperature of the smoked halibut has reached 145°F (63°C). The smoked halibut will flake once it is done.
9. Meanwhile, combine the dip ingredients in a bowl. Place tahini paste and mayonnaise in a bowl then pour lemon juice and vegetable oil over the paste. Stir until incorporated.
10. Once the smoked halibut is done, remove from the wood pellet smoker and transfer to a serving dish.
11. Serve the smoked halibut with tahini dip. Enjoy!

Spiced Smoked Catfish Oregano

(Cooking Time 2 Hours 30 Minutes)

Ingredients for 10 Servings

- Catfish fillet (4-lbs., 1.8-kg.)

The Marinade

- Vegetable oil – 2 cups
- Red Wine Vinegar – ¾ cup
- Lemon juice – 3 tablespoons
- Minced garlic – 2 tablespoons
- Oregano – 2 tablespoons
- Thyme – 1 ½ tablespoons
- Basil – 1 tablespoon
- Black pepper – 1 ½ teaspoons
- Cayenne pepper – 1 teaspoon
- Salt – 1 ½ tablespoons
- Sugar – ¼ cup

The Heat

- Alder wood pellets

Method

1. Pour vegetable oil and red wine vinegar in a bowl.
2. Add minced garlic, oregano, thyme, basil, black pepper, cayenne pepper, salt, and sugar to the bowl then stir in lemon juice. Mix until incorporated.
3. Place the catfish fillet in a baking dish then pour marinade over the catfish.
4. Rub the catfish with the marinade mixture and make sure that the catfish fillet is completely coated. Let the catfish rest for approximately an hour and store in the fridge to keep it fresh.
5. After an hour, take the catfish fillet out of the fridge and thaw at room temperature.

6. Plug the wood pellet smoker and place wood pellet inside the hopper. Turn the switch on.
7. Set the “Smoke” setting and prepare the wood pellet smoker for indirect heat.
8. Wait until the wood pellet smoker is ready then place the seasoned catfish in the wood pellet smoker. Smoke for approximately 30 minutes.
9. Adjust the temperature to 225°F (107°C) and continue smoking the catfish for approximately 2 hours or until the internal temperature has reached 145°F (63°C).
10. Once it is done, remove the smoked catfish from the wood pellet smoker and place on a serving dish.
11. Serve and enjoy.

Chapter-7 SEAFOOD

Smoked Shrimps Teriyaki

(COOKING TIME 10 MINUTES)

INGREDIENTS FOR 10 SERVINGS

- Fresh Shrimps (2-lbs., 0.9-kg.)

THE RUB

- Onion powder – ¾ teaspoon
- Garlic powder – ¾ teaspoon
- Salt – ½ teaspoon

THE GLAZE

- Soy sauce – ¼ cup
- Brown sugar – 2 tablespoons
- Honey – ¾ tablespoon
- Ginger – ½ teaspoon
- Garlic powder – ½ teaspoon

THE HEAT

- Mesquites wood pellets

METHOD

1. Peel the fresh shrimps and discard the head. Let the tails remain.
2. Rub the shrimps with onion powder, garlic powder, and salt then place in a disposable aluminum pan.
3. Next, combine soy sauce with brown sugar, honey, ginger, and garlic powder then stir the sauce ingredients until incorporated.
4. Drizzle the sauce mixture over the shrimps then carefully toss until the shrimps are coated with the liquid.

5. Plug the wood pellet smoker and place wood pellet inside the hopper. Turn the switch on.
6. Set the "Smoke" setting and prepare the wood pellet smoker for indirect heat.
7. Adjust the temperature to 375°F (191°C) and place the aluminum pan with seasoned shrimps inside in the wood pellet smoker.
8. Smoke the shrimps for 10 minutes then remove from the wood pellet smoker.
9. Transfer the smoked shrimps to a serving dish then enjoy.

Citrus Paprika Smoked Lobster Tails with Butter

(Cooking Time 1 Hour 15 Minutes)

Ingredients for 10 Servings

- Lobster tails (3-lbs., 1.4-kg.)

The Glaze

- Butter – ¼ cup
- Minced garlic – 2 tablespoons
- Lemon juice – 3 tablespoons
- Grated lemon zest – ½ teaspoon
- Smoked paprika – 1 teaspoon
- Salt – ¼ teaspoon

The Heat

- Alder wood pellets

Method

1. Melt butter then season with minced garlic, lemon juice, grated lemon zest, smoked paprika, and salt. Stir the butter mixture until incorporated.
2. Cut the shells of the lobster tails then carefully scoop around the inside of each lobster tail to loosen the lobster meat a bit.
3. Next, plug the wood pellet smoker and place wood pellet inside the hopper. Turn the switch on.
4. Set the "Smoke" setting and prepare the wood pellet smoker for indirect heat.
5. Once the wood pellet smoker is ready, arrange the lobster tails in the smoker and drizzle the butter mixture into the cracked shells lobster tails.
6. Smoke the lobster tails for approximately an hour or until the internal temperature has reached 145°F (63°C). Add more time if it is necessary.
7. Once it is finished, take the smoked lobster tails out of the wood pellet smoker and arrange on a serving dish.
8. Serve and enjoy warm.

Tasty Smoked Scallops with Citrus Creamy Sauce

(Cooking Time 45 Minutes)

Ingredients for 10 servings

- Scallops (3.5-lbs., 1.6-kg.)

The Brine

- Water – 1 ½ quarts
- Salt – ¾ cup
- Sugar – ¾ cup
- Soy sauce – ¾ cup
- Grated lemon zest – 2 teaspoons
- Bay leaves – 2
- Dried dill weed – ¾ tablespoon

The Sauce

- Salted butter – ½ cup
- Garlic powder – 1 tablespoon
- Grated orange zest – ½ teaspoon
- Orange juice – ¼ cup
- Worcestershire sauce – ¼ teaspoon
- Chopped tarragon – ½ teaspoon
- Chopped parsley – 1 teaspoon

The Heat

- Alder wood pellets

Method

1. Add salt, sugar, soy sauce, grated lemon zest, bay leaves, and dried dill weed to the water then stir the mixture until incorporated.
2. Stir in the scallops to the brine mixture then soak for approximately an hour.
3. After an hour, take the scallops out of the brine then wash and rinse them.
4. Plug the wood pellet smoker and place wood pellet inside the hopper. Turn the switch on.
5. Set the "Smoke" setting and prepare the wood pellet smoker for indirect heat.
6. Adjust the temperature to 200°F (93°C) and smoke the scallops for 45 minutes.
7. In the meantime, melt the salted butter then stir garlic powder, grated lemon zest, and Worcestershire sauce.
8. Pour orange juice into the butter mixture then stir until incorporated.
9. Add chopped tarragon and parsley to the sauce then mix well. Remove from heat and let it cool.
10. Once the smoked scallops are done, take them out of the wood pellet smoker and transfer to a serving dish.
11. Serve with the sauce and enjoy immediately.

Smoked Sweet Prawn Spicy Garlic

(Cooking Time 30 Minutes)

Ingredients for 10 Servings

- Large Prawns (2-lbs., 0.9-kg.)

The Rub

- Brown sugar – ½ cup
- Salt – 1 tablespoon
- Paprika – 2 ½ teaspoons
- Chili powder – 1 ½ teaspoons
- Garlic powder – 2 teaspoons
- Onion powder – 2 teaspoons

The Heat

- Apple wood pellets

Method

1. Combine the rub ingredients—brown sugar, salt, paprika, chili powder, garlic powder, and onion powder in a container then stir the mixture well.
2. Add prawns to the container then cover with the lid.
3. Toss the prawns to season then marinate for an hour. Store in the fridge to keep it fresh.
4. After an hour, take the container out of the fridge and thaw the prawns at room temperature.
5. Plug the wood pellet smoker and place wood pellet inside the hopper. Turn the switch on.
6. Set the "Smoke" setting and prepare the wood pellet smoker for indirect heat. Adjust the temperature to 200°F (93°C).
7. Using wood pellet smoker skewers prick the prawns and place in the wood pellet smoker.

8. Smoke the prawns for approximately 30 minutes or until smoked prawns are opaque and turn to pink.
9. Once it is done, remove the smoked prawns from the wood pellet smoker and arrange on a serving dish.
10. Serve and enjoy.

Natural Juicy Smoked Oyster with Sunflower Oil

(Cooking Time 2 Hours 5 Minutes)

Ingredients for 10 servings

- Fresh Oyster without Shells (2-lbs., 0.9-kg.)

The Rub

- Salt – ½ teaspoon
- Sunflower oil – 3 tablespoons
- Lemon juice – 2 tablespoons

The Heat

- Cherry wood pellets

Method

1. Place the oysters in a disposable aluminum pan then rub the oyster with salt, sunflower oil, and lemon juice.
2. Plug the wood pellet smoker and place wood pellet inside the hopper. Turn the switch on.
3. Set the "Smoke" setting and prepare the wood pellet smoker for indirect heat.
4. Adjust the temperature to 175°F (80°C) and place the aluminum pan with oysters in the wood pellet smoker.
5. Smoke the oysters for 2 hours or until tender.
6. Once it is done, remove from the wood pellet smoker and transfer to a serving dish.
7. Serve the smoked oysters on top of biscuits then enjoy!

Chapter-8 GAME

Aromatic Smoked Duck Breast Paprika Basils

(Cooking Time 3 Hours 10 Minutes)

Ingredients for 10 Servings

- Duck breast (3-lbs., 1.4kg.)

The Marinade

- Apple juice – 3 cups
- Salt – 1 tablespoon
- Sugar – 1 ½ tablespoons
- Soy sauce – 2 tablespoons
- Paprika – ¾ teaspoon
- Garlic powder – ¾ teaspoon
- Dried basils – 1 teaspoon
- Pepper – ¾ teaspoon

The Heat

- Cherry wood pellets

Method

1. Pour apple juice into a container then season with salt, sugar, soy sauce, paprika, garlic powder, dried basils, and pepper. Stir the liquid until incorporated.
2. Score the duck breast at several places then put the duck breast into the marinade. Marinade the duck breast for 4 hours and store in the refrigerator to keep it fresh.

3. Plug the wood pellet smoker and place wood pellet inside the hopper. Turn the switch on.
4. Set the "Smoke" setting and prepare the wood pellet smoker for indirect heat.
5. Adjust the temperature to 325°F (163°C) and wait until the wood pellet smoker has reached the desired temperature.
6. Remove the duck breast from the refrigerator then take it out from the marinade. Place the seasoned duck breast in the wood pellet smoker.
7. Once the internal temperature of the duck breast has reached 135°F (57°C), remove from the wood pellet smoker and transfer to a serving dish.
8. Cut the smoked duck breast into thick slices then serve.
9. Enjoy!

Lemon Honey Smoked Rabbit Barbecue

(Cooking Time 2 Hours 15 Minutes)

Ingredients for 10 Servings

- Rabbit (6-lbs., 2.7-kg.)

The Rub

- Paprika – ¼ cup
- Brown sugar – 2 tablespoons
- White sugar – 2 tablespoons
- Salt – 1 tablespoon
- Black pepper – 2 teaspoons
- Cayenne – 1 ½ teaspoons
- Dry mustard – 2 teaspoons
- Garlic powder – 2 teaspoons
- Onion powder – 2 teaspoons

The Glaze

- Lemon juice – ¼ cup
- Honey – ½ cup
- Olive oil – ¼ cup
- Thyme – 1 teaspoon
- Rosemary – ¾ teaspoon
- Garlic powder – 1 teaspoon
- Black pepper – ½ teaspoon

The Heat

- Apple wood pellets

METHOD

1. Combine the rub ingredients—paprika, brown sugar, white sugar, salt, black pepper, cayenne, dry mustard, garlic powder, and onion powder in a bowl then stir the spices until mixed.
2. Rub the rabbit with the spice mixture then let it rest for approximately 2 hours. Cover with plastic wrap and store in the fridge to keep it fresh.
3. After 2 hours, plug the wood pellet smoker and place wood pellet inside the hopper. Turn the switch on.
4. Set the "Smoke" setting and prepare the wood pellet smoker for indirect heat.
5. Adjust the temperature to 300°F (149°C) and wait until the wood pellet smoker has reached the desired temperature.
6. Once the wood pellet smoker is ready, unwrap the rabbit and place in the wood pellet smoker. Smoke the rabbit for an hour.
7. In the meantime, pour lemon juice, honey, and olive oil in a bowl then season with thyme, rosemary, garlic powder, and black pepper. Stir the glaze mixture until incorporated.
8. After an hour of smoking, baste the rabbit with the glaze mixture then continue smoking for another hour.
9. Once the internal temperature of the smoked rabbit has reached 165°F (74°C), remove from the wood pellet smoker and place on a sheet of aluminum foil.
10. Baste the smoked rabbit with the remaining glaze mixture then wrap with the foil. Let it rest for 15 minutes.
11. Unwrap the smoked rabbit then place on a serving dish.
12. Cut into thick slices then serve.
13. Enjoy!

Aromatic Pineapple Smoked Cornish Tender

(Cooking Time 1 Hour 10 Minutes)

Ingredients for 10 Servings

- 2 Whole cornish (5-lbs., 2.3-kg.)

The Marinade

- Pineapple chunks – 2 cups
- Brown sugar – 3 tablespoons
- Garlic powder – 1 tablespoon
- Ginger powder – 1 teaspoon
- Cloves – a pinch
- Apple cider vinegar – ¼ cup
- Lemon juice – 2 tablespoons

The Glaze

- Honey – ½ cup
- Olive oil – 2 tablespoons

The Heat

- Hickory wood pellets

Method

1. Place pineapple chunks, brown sugar, garlic powder, ginger powder, cloves, apple cider vinegar, and lemon juice in a blender. Blend the mixture until smooth and incorporated.
2. Season the Cornish with the pineapple mixture then marinate overnight. Store in the fridge to keep it fresh.
3. In the morning, remove the Cornish from the fridge and thaw at room temperature.

4. Plug the wood pellet smoker and place wood pellet inside the hopper. Turn the switch on.
5. Set the "Smoke" setting and prepare the wood pellet smoker for indirect heat.
6. When the smoke is ready, set the temperature to 275°F (135°C) and wait until the wood pellet smoker has reached the desired temperature.
7. Quickly stir honey with olive oil then baste the mixture over the Cornish.
8. Place the Cornish in the wood pellet smoker then smoke for an hour or until the internal temperature has reached 165°F (74°C).
9. Remove the smoked Cornish from the wood pellet smoker and transfer to a serving dish.
10. Serve and enjoy!

Juicy Smoked Venison Tender with Simple Spices

(COOKING TIME 1 HOUR 10 MINUTES)

INGREDIENTS FOR 10 SERVINGS

- Venison tenderloin (4-lbs., 1.8-kg.)

THE INJECTION

- Beef stock – 1 ½ cups
- Garlic powder – 1 teaspoon
- Pepper – ½ teaspoon
- Worcestershire sauce – 2 tablespoons

THE RUB

- Chili powder – ¼ cup
- Salt – 1 tablespoon
- Garlic powder – 3 tablespoons
- Onion powder – 3 tablespoons
- Black pepper – 2 tablespoons
- Brown sugar – 3 tablespoons
- Dry mustard – 1 tablespoon

THE HEAT

- Hickory wood pellets

METHOD

1. Season the beef stock with garlic powder, pepper, and Worcestershire sauce then stir until incorporated.
2. Fill an injector with the beef stock mixture then inject the venison tenderloin at several places.
3. Plug the wood pellet smoker and place wood pellet inside the hopper. Turn the switch on.

4. Set the "Smoke" setting and prepare the wood pellet smoker for indirect heat.
5. Adjust the temperature to 400°F (204°C) and wait until the wood pellet smoker is ready.
6. Combine the rub ingredients—chili powder, salt, garlic powder, onion powder, black pepper, brown sugar, and dry mustard in a bowl. Stir the spices until combined.
7. Rub the venison tenderloin with the spice mixture then place in the wood pellet smoker.
8. Smoke the venison for approximately an hour or until the internal temperature has reached 165°F (74°C).
9. If you want to have medium-rare doneness, smoke the venison until the internal temperature has reached 145°F (63°C).
10. Once the smoked venison is done, remove from the wood pellet smoker and transfer to a serving dish.
11. Cut into thick slices then serve.
12. Enjoy!

Tropical Citrus Smoked Quails in Lemon Orange Marinade

(Cooking Time 1 Hours 10 Minutes)

Ingredients for 10 Servings

- Quails (5-lbs., 2.3-kg.)

The Marinade

- Orange juice – 2 cups
- Soy sauce – 1 cup
- Minced garlic – 2 tablespoons
- Brown sugar – ½ cup
- Olive oil – ¼ cup
- Black pepper – 1 tablespoon
- Chopped onion – 1 cup

The Heat

- Alder wood pellets

Method

1. Pour orange juice into a container then add soy sauce, minced garlic, brown sugar, olive oil, black pepper, and chopped onion. Stir the mixture until combined.
2. Add quails to the container then toss to coat.
3. Cover the container with the lid and marinate the quails for at least 3 hours. Marinate the quails overnight is also fine.
4. Plug the wood pellet smoker and place wood pellet inside the hopper. Turn the switch on.
5. Set the "Smoke" setting and prepare the wood pellet smoker for indirect heat.
6. Adjust the temperature to 225°F (107°C) and place the marinated quails in the wood pellet smoker with the breast side up.
7. Smoke the quails for an hour or until the smoke quails are firm and the internal temperature has reached 145°F (63°C).
8. Once it is done, remove the smoked quails to a serving dish then serve.
9. Enjoy.

Chapter-9
VEGETABLES

Sweet Crispy Smoked Carrot with Cinnamon Maple Glaze

(Cooking Time 40 Minutes)

Ingredients for 10 servings

- Fresh Carrots (2-lbs., 0.9-kg.)

The Rub

- Salt – ¼ teaspoon
- Pepper – ½ teaspoon
- Brown sugar – 2 tablespoons
- Olive oil – 3 tablespoons

The Glaze

- Maple syrup – ¼ cup
- Cinnamon – 1 teaspoon
- Brown sugar – 2 tablespoons

The Heat

- Maple wood pellets

METHOD

1. Combine olive oil with salt, pepper and brown sugar then stir the mixture until mixed.
2. Choose medium to large carrots then peel them. Cut into quarters lengthwise.
3. Rub the carrots with the spice mixture then place in a bowl. Let the carrots rest for 10 minutes.
4. Plug the wood pellet smoker and place wood pellet inside the hopper. Turn the switch on.
5. Set the "Smoke" setting and prepare the wood pellet smoker for indirect heat.
6. Adjust the temperature to 400°F (204°C) and wait until the wood pellet smoker has reached the desired temperature.
7. While waiting for the smoke, drizzle maple syrup over the carrots then toss to coat.
8. Roll the carrots in the brown sugar and cinnamon mixture then place in the wood pellet smoker.
9. Smoke the carrots for approximately 20 to 30 minutes or until the carrots are tender enough.
10. Remove the smoked carrots from the wood pellet smoker and transfer to a serving dish.
11. Serve and enjoy.

Smoked Stuffed Tomato Cheese

(Cooking Time 1 Hours 45 Minutes)

Ingredients for 10 Servings

- Fresh Red Tomatoes (1.5-lbs., 0.7kg.)

The Filling

- Breadcrumbs – 1 cup
- Grated cheddar cheese – 1 cup
- Grated Mozzarella cheese – ¾ cup
- Black pepper – ½ teaspoon
- Nutmeg – ¼ teaspoon

The Heat

- Alder wood pellets

Method

1. Choose big red tomatoes then cut the top of the tomatoes.
2. Scoop out the inside of the tomatoes then arrange on a flat surface.
3. Combine breadcrumbs with grated cheddar cheese then fill each tomato with the mixture.
4. Sprinkle grated mozzarella cheese on top then dust with black pepper.
5. Plug the wood pellet smoker and place wood pellet inside the hopper. Turn the switch on.
6. Set the "Smoke" setting and prepare the wood pellet smoker for indirect heat.
7. Adjust the temperature to 225°F (107°C) and wait until the wood pellet smoker has reached the desired temperature.
8. When the smoke is ready, arrange the stuffed tomatoes directly in the wood pellet smoker and smoke for an hour and a half. The smoked tomatoes will look wilted and the cheese will melt.
9. Once it is done, remove the smoked stuffed tomatoes from the wood pellet smoker and arrange on a serving dish.
10. Serve and enjoy.

Spicy Smoked Onion with Taco Seasoning

(COOKING TIME 2 HOURS 5 MINUTES)

INGREDIENTS FOR 10 SERVINGS

- Onions (1-lb., 0.5-kg.)

THE SEASONING

- Olive oil – 1 ½ tablespoons
- Chili powder – 1 ½ teaspoons
- Cumin – 1 teaspoon
- Paprika – ½ teaspoon
- Salt – ½ teaspoon
- Garlic powder – ½ teaspoon
- Onion powder – ½ teaspoon
- Oregano – ¼ teaspoon
- Black pepper – ¼ teaspoon

THE HEAT

- Apple wood pellets

METHOD

1. Combine chili powder with cumin, paprika, salt, garlic powder, onion powder, oregano, and black pepper then stir the spices until mixed.
2. Cut the hard part on the onions on the top then discard the outer layer of the onions.
3. Brush olive oil over each onion then liberally sprinkle the spice mixture over the onions.
4. Plug the wood pellet smoker and place wood pellet inside the hopper. Turn the switch on.
5. Set the "Smoke" setting and prepare the wood pellet smoker for indirect heat.

6. Adjust the temperature to 225°F (107°C) and once it reaches the desired temperature, arrange the onions in the wood pellet smoker.
7. Smoke the onions for 2 hours or more if you want to have smokier aroma and flavor.
8. Once it is done, remove the smoked onions from the wood pellet smoker and arrange on a serving dish.
9. Cut the smoked onions into slices then serve.
10. Enjoy!

Smoked Butternut Squash with Honey and Maple Glaze

(Cooking Time 1 Hour 40 Minutes)

Ingredients for 10 Servings

- Butternut Squash (3-lbs., 1.4-kg.)

The Rub

- Olive oil – 2 ½ tablespoons
- Salt – ½ teaspoon
- Black pepper – ½ teaspoon
- Garlic powder ½ teaspoon
- Brown sugar – 1 ½ teaspoons
- Chili powder – ½ tablespoon

The Glaze

- Maple syrup – ½ cup
- Honey – 2 tablespoons
- Butter – 2 tablespoons
- Chili powder – ½ teaspoon

The Heat

- Maple wood pellets

Method

1. Peel the butternut squash then cut into halves lengthwise.
2. Score the butternut squash and make the crisscrossing diagonal length.
3. Brush with olive oil then sprinkle salt, black pepper, garlic powder, brown sugar, and chili powder over the butternut squash.
4. Plug the wood pellet smoker and place wood pellet inside the hopper. Turn the switch on.
5. Set the "Smoke" setting and prepare the wood pellet smoker for indirect heat.

6. Adjust the temperature to 325°F (163°C) and wait until the wood pellet smoker is ready.
7. Melt butter then combine with maple syrup, honey, and chili powder. Stir the liquid until incorporated.
8. Glaze the butternut squash with the maple syrup and honey mixture then place in the wood pellet smoker.
9. Smoke the butternut squash for approximately an hour and a half or until the smoked butternut squash has reached the desired softness.
10. Remove the smoked butternut squash from the wood pellet smoker and transfer to a serving dish.
11. Quickly glaze again the smoked butternut squash with the maple syrup and honey mixture then serve.
12. Enjoy!

Tasty Smoked Cabbage Barbecue Butter

(Cooking Time 4 Hours 10 Minutes)

Ingredients for 10 Servings

- Whole Cabbage (2-lbs., 0.9-kg.)

The Glaze

- Ketchup – 1 cup
- Brown sugar – ¼ cup
- Molasses – 3 tablespoons
- Pineapple juice – ¼ cup
- Worcestershire sauce – ¾ tablespoon
- Mustard – 2 tablespoons
- Smoked paprika – 1 ½ teaspoons
- Garlic powder – ½ teaspoon
- Cayenne pepper – ¼ teaspoon
- Salt – ½ teaspoon
- Pepper – ½ teaspoon

The Filling

- Butter – ¼ cup
- Canola oil – ¼ cup

The Heat

- Maple wood pellets

Method

1. Pour ketchup into a saucepan then add brown sugar, molasses, pineapple juice, Worcestershire sauce, mustard, smoked paprika, garlic powder, cayenne pepper, salt, and pepper.

2. Stir the mixture then bring to a simmer over low heat.
3. Remove the barbecue sauce from the heat and let it cool for a few minutes.
4. Plug the wood pellet smoker and place wood pellet inside the hopper. Turn the switch on.
5. Set the "Smoke" setting and prepare the wood pellet smoker for indirect heat.
6. Adjust the temperature to 225°F (107°C) and wait until the smoke is ready.
7. Cut the top of the cabbage then place it in a disposable aluminum pan with the cavity of the cabbage facing up.
8. Baste the cabbage with the barbecue sauce then place in the wood pellet smoker.
9. Smoke the cabbage for 2 hours and baste with the barbecue sauce once every 30 minutes.
10. After 2 hours, increase the temperature to 325°F (163°C) and take the cabbage out of the wood pellet smoker.
11. Baste the cabbage with the remaining barbecue sauce then wrap with aluminum foil but leave the top of the cabbage open.
12. Melt butter over low heat then combine with canola oil. Stir the liquid until incorporated.
13. Carefully drizzle the butter mixture over the cabbage and let it goes in between the cabbage leaves.
14. Return the cabbage to the wood pellet smoker and smoke for another 2 hours.
15. Once the smoked cabbage is done, remove from the wood pellet smoker and let it cool for a few minutes.
16. Unwrap the smoked cabbage then cut into one-bite sizes.
17. Arrange the smoked cabbage on a serving dish then serve.
18. Enjoy!

Chapter-10 Information on Smoking Meat

What is the primary difference between Barbequing a meat and smoking it?

You might not believe it, but there are still people who think that the process of Barbequing and Smoking are the same! So, this is something which you should know about before diving in deeper.

So, whenever you are going to use a traditional BBQ grill, you always put your meat directly on top of the heat source for a brief amount of time which eventually cooks up the meal. Smoking, on the other hand, will require you to combine the heat from your grill as well as the smoke to infuse a delicious smoky texture and flavor to your meat. Smoking usually takes much longer than traditional barbecuing. In most cases, it takes a minimum of 2 hours and a temperature of 100 -120 degrees for the smoke to be properly infused into the meat. Keep in mind that the time and temperature will obviously depend on the type of meat that you are using, and that is why it is suggested that you keep a meat thermometer handy to ensure that your meat is doing fine. Keep in mind that this method of barbecuing is also known as "Low and slow" smoking as well. With that cleared up, you should be aware that there are actually two different ways through which smoking is done.

The core difference between cold and hot smoking

Depending on the type of grill that you are using, you might be able to get the option to go for a Hot Smoking Method or a Cold Smoking One. The primary fact about these three different cooking techniques which you should keep in mind are as follows:

- **Hot Smoking:** In this technique, the food will use both the heat on your grill and the smoke to prepare your food. This method is most suitable for items such as chicken, lamb, brisket etc.
- **Cold Smoking:** In this method, you are going to smoke your meat at a very low temperature such as 30 degree Celsius, making sure that it doesn't come into the direct contact with the heat. This is mostly used as a means to preserve meat and extend their life on the shelf.
- **Roasting Smoke:** This is also known as Smoke Baking. This process is essentially a combined form of both roasting and baking and can be performed in any type of smoker with a capacity of reaching temperatures above 82 degree Celsius.

By now you must be really curious to know about the different types of Smokers that are out there right?

Well, in the next section I am exactly going to discuss that!

The different types of available Smokers

Essentially, what you should know is that right now in the market, you are going to get three different types of Smokers.

Charcoal Smoker

These types of smokers are hands down the best one for infusing the perfect Smoky flavor to your meat. But be warned, though, that these smokers are a little bit difficult to master as the method of regulating temperature is a little bit difficult when compared to normal Gas or Electric smokers.

Electric Smoker

After the charcoal smoker, next comes perhaps the simpler option, Electric Smokers. These are easy to use and plug and play type. All you need to do is just plug in, set the temperature and go about your daily life. The smoker will do the rest. However, keep in mind that the finishing smoky flavor won't be as intense as the Charcoal one.

Gas Smokers

Finally, comes the Gas Smokers. These have a fairly easy mechanism for temperature control and are powered usually by LP Gas. The drawback of these Smokers is that you are going to have to keep checking up on your Smoker every now and then to ensure that it has not run out of Gas.

Now, these have been further dissected into different styles of the smoker. Each of which is preferred by Smokers of different experiences.

The different styles of smokers

The different styles of Smokers are essentially divided into the following.

Vertical (Bullet Style Using Charcoal)

These are usually low-cost solutions and are perfect for first-time smokers.

Vertical (Cabinet Style)

These Smokers come with a square shaped design with cabinets and drawers/trays for easy accessibility. These cookers also come with a water tray and a designated wood chips box as well.

Offset

These type of smokers have dedicated fireboxes that are attached to the side of the main grill. The smoke and heat required for these are generated from the firebox itself which is then passed through the main chamber and out through a nicely placed chimney.

Kamado Joe

And finally, we have the Kamado Joe which is ceramic smokers are largely regarded as being the "Jack Of All Trades".

These smokers can be used as low and slow smokers, grills, hi or low-temperature ovens and so on.

They have a very thick ceramic wall which allows it to hold heat better than any other type of smoker out there, requiring only a little amount of charcoal.

These are easy to use with better insulation and are more efficient when it comes to fuel control.

With the smokers now set up, the next step is to understand about the woods used in the smoker. Below is a table which discusses most of the general types of woods that are used in Smokers and their potential benefits.

The different types of wood and their benefits

The Different Types Of Wood	Suitable For
Hickory	Wild game, chicken, pork, cheeses, beef
Pecan	Chicken, pork, lamb, cheeses, fish.
Mesquite	Beef and vegetables
Alder	Swordfish, Salmon, Sturgeon and other types of fishes. Works well with pork and chicken too.
Oak	Beef or briskets
Maple	Vegetable, ham or poultry
Cherry	Game birds, poultry or pork
Apple	Game birds, poultry, beef
Peach	Game birds, poultry or pork
Grape Vines	Beef, chicken or turkey
Wine Barrel Chips	Turkey, beef, chicken or cheeses
Seaweed	Lobster, mussels, crab, shrimp etc.
Herbs or Spices such as rosemary, bay leaves, mint, lemon peels, whole nutmeg etc.	Good for cheeses or vegetables and a small collection of light meats such as fillets or fish steaks.

The basic preparations

- Always be prepared to spend the whole day and take as much time as possible to smoke your meat for maximum effect.
- Make sure to obtain the perfect Ribs/Meat for the meal which you are trying to smoke. Do a little bit of research if you need.
- I have already added a list of woods in this book, consult to that list and choose the perfect wood for your meal.
- Make sure to prepare the marinade for each of the meals properly. A great deal of the flavor comes from the rubbing.
- Keep a meat thermometer handy to get the internal temperature when needed.
- Use mittens or tongs to keep yourself safe
- Refrain yourself from using charcoal infused alongside starter fluid as it might bring a very unpleasant odor to your food
- Always make sure to start off with a small amount of wood and keep adding them as you cook.
- Don't be afraid to experiment with different types of wood for newer flavor and experiences.
- Always keep a notebook near you and note jot down whatever you are doing or learning and use them during the future session. This will help you to evolve and move forward.

The core elements of smoking!

Smoking is a very indirect method of cooking that relies on a number of different factors to give you the most perfectly cooked meal that you are looking for. Each of these components is very important to the whole process as they all work together to create the meal of your dreams.

- **Time**: Unlike grilling or even Barbequing, smoking takes a really long time and requires a whole lot of patience. It takes time for the smoky flavor to slowly get infused into the meats. Jus to bring things into comparison, it takes an about 8 minutes to fully cook a steak through direct heating, while smoking (indirect heating) will take around 35-40 minutes.
- **Temperature:** When it comes to smoking, the temperature is affected by a lot of different factors that are not only limited to the wind, cold air temperatures but also the cooking wood's dryness. Some smokers work best with large fires that are controlled by the draw of a chimney and restricted airflow through the various vents of the cooking chamber and firebox. While other smokers tend to require smaller fire with fewer coals as well as a completely different combination of the vent and draw controls. However, most smokers are designed to work at temperatures as low as 180 degrees Fahrenheit to as high as 300 degrees Fahrenheit. But the recommend temperature usually falls between 250 degrees Fahrenheit and 275 degrees Fahrenheit.
- **Airflow:** The level of air to which the fire is exposed to greatly determines how your fire will burn and how quickly it will burn the fuel. For instance, if you restrict air flow into the firebox by closing up the available vents, then the fire will burn at a low temperature and vice versa. Typically in smokers, after lighting up the fire, the vents are opened to allow for maximum air flow and is then adjusted throughout the cooking process to make sure that optimum flame is achieved.
- **Insulation:** Insulation is also very important when it comes to smokers as it helps to easily manage the cooking process throughout the whole cooking session. A good insulation allows smokers to efficiently reach the desired temperature instead of waiting for hours upon hours!

CPSIA information can be obtained
at www.ICGtesting.com
Printed in the USA
LVHW101648160820
663340LV00022B/522

9 781649 840752